Hey, it's Me….

Bert Corbeil

Copyright © 2025 Bert Corbeil

All rights reserved. De Colores Publishing

Denver, Colorado

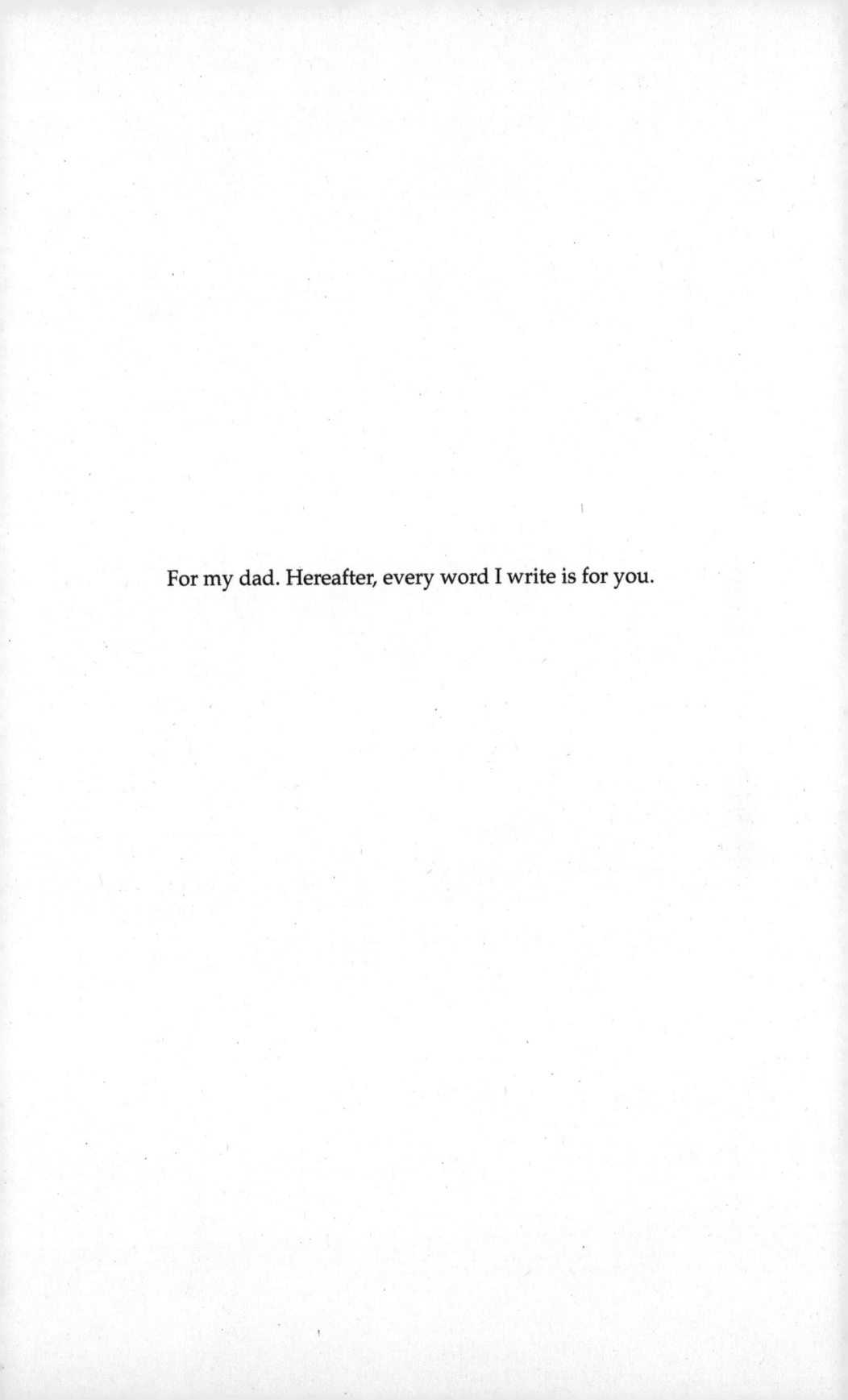

For my dad. Hereafter, every word I write is for you.

Also by Bert Corbeil
Chaos Under The Moon

CONTENTS

Earlier 15
A Visit 17
Inner Turmoil 19
For Someone 21
A Family 23
A Poem From the Point of View of My Cat
                                         25
Pictures of Moments 27
Vacation 29
On The Screen 31
Dig Deep 33
Chapped 35
More Than Touch 37
Oh child, ... 39
My Garden 41
Now 43
Babylon 45
Breathe & Repeat 47
Child-Like Wonder 49
Returned 51
Strangers Apart 53
Day One 55
With Night 57
The Moon as a Witness 59
I Sit 61

A Wonderful Thing	63
Changing Direction	65
Frolicking Souls	67
An Instant Worth Saving	69
When Avalon Wrote	71
For The Love	73
The End of The Line	75
Crumbs	77
Wading	79
Meeting Again	81
Your Green Pearls	83
Sleep Less	85
Dancing on Air	87
Companion	89
Drunk with Static	91
Endless Versions	93
Like A House	95
Different Lands	97
How Does a Frog Find its Home	99
Ahead	101
Initial Reaction	103
I'll be Waiting	105
Airplane Thoughts	107
Unorganized Grief	109
An Easy Breeze	111
Called Love	113

Balancing Each Other ... 115
The Light ... 117
A Conversation With Myself ... 119

Hey, It's Me…

Bert Corbeil

EARLIER

If it wasn't for you I'd be gone
I was going through life feeling like a pawn
But you gave me hope and direction
You gave me all of your affection
Even when your mind wasn't whole
You gave purpose for my soul
Lately my days have been
filled with yawns
Ever since you've been gone

Bert Corbeil

EARLIER

It it wasn't to you I'd be wed,
I was somethimes though there was hope
But you gave me hope and direction
You gave me all of your affection
Even when you might well not whole
You gave comfort for my soul
Lately my days have been
filled with sorrow
Ever since you've been gone

A VISIT

Occasionally, you visit me in my dreams.
Every time it feels real.
In the dreams, we are driving,
I don't care where,
You talk to me you were never sick,
And I just listen,
You talk and talk,
and i hope you never stop,
But then I wake up,
And I am back in a world
 where you are forever gone.
These dreams may seem cruel,
But they bring me joy,
They bring back the moments I miss.
You are always welcome to visit, grandpa.

Bert Corbeil

A VISIT

Occasionally, you visit me in my dreams,
Everyminute feels real.
In the dreams, we are driving,
I don't care where.
You talk to me, you were never sick,
And I just listen.
You talk and talk,
And I hope you never stop.
But then I wake up,
And I am back in a world
where you are forever gone.
These dreams may seem cruel,
But they bring me joy.
They hand back the moments I miss.
You are always welcome to visit, grandpa.

INNER TURMOIL

To people who think my life is together,
I experience panic attacks
that leave me weathered.
Brought upon by thoughts of
unsubstantial judgments from others.
Lies of not being enough force me
 to hide under the covers.
I spend sleepless nights
wondering if I'll make it past thirty,
And if I do, will my life even be sturdy?
All these anxieties make it hard
 for me to enjoy things,
The only real enemy that I have
 is myself.

FOR SOMEONE

I want someone to feel what I feel.
Someone to let me know I am not alone,
To let me know what I feel is normal.
I want someone to comfort me
and reassure me the world is not over.
Someone who can be my crutch
when I am too weak to walk.
Someone to guide when it gets too dark.
Someone to squeeze my hand
when fear becomes too powerful.
Someone who won't give up when things get hard.
Someone who i can just talk to
and know everything will be okay,
In return,
I'll be that someone for them.

Bert Corbeil

A FAMILY

To be a family, you need togetherness,
Otherwise you're just a bunch of strangers
living under the same roof.
You don't have to be related by blood,
All you need is stability, and care for another.
Family, whoever they may be,
are the ones who will stick with you.
These are the ones you can rely on,
The ones you can trust with anything.
Family is the bond stronger than blood.

Bert Corbeil

A FAMILY

To be a family, you need togetherness,
Otherwise, you're just a bunch of strangers
living under the same roof.
You don't have to be related by blood,
All you need is nobility and care for another.
Family, whoever they may be,
are the ones who will stick with you.
These are the ones you can rely on.
The ones you can trust with anything.
Family is the bond stronger than blood.

A POEM FROM THE POINT OF VIEW OF MY CAT

The sky is after me,
I can feel it.
The clouds are angry,
And I am all alone.
They are bombing the earth,
Boom. Boom. Boom.

I try to get to the basement,
I'll be safe there.
I fight to get the door open,
But something is blocking it,
And I am no longer alone,
I feel them getting closer.
BOOM. BOOM. BOOM.

Getting louder and louder.
I agitate and finally get the door to open.
I run downstairs,
And suddenly I feel at ease.
Minutes pass,
Maybe hours.

It's quiet.
The sky has retreated.

Bert Corbeil

I sneak back upstairs,
Return to my chair,
And resume my bath.

PICTURES OF MOMENTS

I wish more pictures were taken of me,
So I can never lose sight of who I was,
Of who I am.
I want to always remember my moments,
The ones that challenge me,
The ones that change me.
I want proof I lived a life worth living,
Proof I laughed,
Proof I loved.
I never want to forget the child I was,
The man I am now,
And the person I will become.

Bert Corbeil

PICTURES OF MOMENTS

I wish more pictures were taken of me
So I can never lose sight of what I was
Of who I am.
I want to always remember my tofone of
The faces that challenge me,
The ones that change me.
I want proof I lived it life worthliving
Proof I laughed,
Proof I cried.
I never want to forget the child I was,
The man I am now
And the person I will become.

VACATION

This place exudes a certain quietness I've never heard before
I only hear my thoughts dissipating.
From the back porch
I see the grass pushing through the stones
Fighting for the light, fighting to live
I see the dead trees growing back their leaves
Returning to their buoyant forms
I see the water resembling sand glass
Only being interrupted by a few excited fish
I see the homes across the lake mingling with nature
I smell only the scents that travel from neighboring life
I feel my muscles relax as my toes tap on the wood
I feel my body calm as my breath leaves the shallows
I feel this moment wait for as long as it can

Hey, it's Me...

ON THE SCREEN

My head unwinds on her thigh
As she sits up straight reading the TV
My toes find their way under the cushion, finding warmth
The tension in my back spills into the couch
Her fingers carouse in my hair
While our eyes and minds obsess over the drama on the screen
Loss and sorrow gloss in the scene
In a picture we've seen before
But one that never wears it's welcome
My lips follow the words shooting out the screen
Until the next transition
Until my eyes wander up
And decide to watch the curve of her bottom lip
It moves so slightly from her breathing
Matching the slow intensity of the plot
I savor the wonder in her eyes as the film beckons
My hand reaches to feel the expression etched on her face
My index slides under her ear
Pushing back her short, brown hair
My thumb slides across her cheek
As her attention leaves the screen
And travels elsewhere

Hey, it's Me...

DIG DEEP

Give me a chance
And learn every part of me
If you don't like the surface
Pare my skin until you reach the other layers
Shoot to my brain
And linger in my frontal lobe
Expand through me
Flirt with the weaknesses inside my bones
Skim through my nerves as if they're pages in a manual
At least mess with my heart before you finish the tour
Risk what you know

Put me to the test
Crack me open beyond my limits
Play with my pain
If you choose to stay

Bert Corbeil

DIG DEEP

Give me a chance
And learn once and for all.
If you don't close the shutter,
Bare my skin until you reach the other layers
Shoot to my brain
And finger in my harmful folds.
Expand through me.
Him with the red roses under his hoof,
Slash through my nerves as if they're rages in thousand
At least mess with my heart before you finish the rope.
Risk what you know.

Put me to the test.
Crack me open beyond my limits.
Play with my guns.
If you'd bother to stop.

34

CHAPPED

Chapped lips in darkness.
It burns like a small, dying flame.
But the flame never dies.
I want to close my eyes and doze;
Instead I have 'what could be' on my mind.
What could be with you,
With us,
With me.
My mind's library loses its order and explodes;
Leaving millions of ink covered pages lying
around the basement of my brain with
no one to pick them up.
The flame continues.
As 'what could be' continues,
'What is' begins to stomp its feet.
It wants attention.
What are you?
What are we?
What am I?
I'm too afraid to answer these on my own.
But in my brain they will stick,
Until I feel the moment calls for their arrival.
I dampen my lips to extinguish the flame
Darkness becomes morning.

All of me finally grows tired.
The thoughts continue in my dreams.
I take their suffering.
I know I can outlast them,
Like chapped lips in darkness.

MORE THAN TOUCH

I want to be touched by love.
I want to feel its beats and rhythms;
Its idiosyncrasies that come with individuals.
I want to feel someone's incomparable love.
I want to avoid being told about love.
I don't want to hear I'm loved by an empty vessel;
One that has no intent in showing that love.
Do not tell me you love me unless you mean it.
I want to feel the body of love,
The allure of it,
Be entranced by it.
I want to embrace the toes,
The neck,
The belly,
The eyes of it.
I want it to be true,
Like the fear of losing something.
I want it to be reckless:
Fast and slow,
Hard and soft,
Clear and foggy,
Pain and joy.
Oh, how I desire the touch of love.

OH CHILD,

I don't want you to have my strength;
I hope you are stronger.
My strength is wrapped in bandages
with scars bleeding through.
There's nothing more I desire than for your strength
 to require no such remedy.
Please gather life's wisdoms quicker than I ever could.
I want you to grow taller than me;
Learn that I won't always be right.
Listen to everything you hear and keep
the things you think will help you along.
It's okay to be confused and lost;
Just, don't think you have to find your way
only on your own.
It takes great strength to lean on someone's shoulder.;
It takes great strength to be
the one that owns that shoulder also.
I want you not to live in any shadow;
Hold your head higher than I ever could.
I don't want you to be afraid of your emotions;
I'll guide you in finding your courage.
I want you to know that I will always listen to you;
I understand that you are your own self.
I understand that you will have your own ideas;
your own passions.

I also understand that you will face your obstacles and failures.
You will get sad,
You will get angry,
You will fill with fear;
Sometimes all at once.
At your darkest moments, just remember
 it is not the end of the world;
Your world will never crumble beyond repair,
this I promise.
It's okay to misplace hope and love;
Just be sure to find them in the end.
We will have fights.
We will have disagreements.
But please never stop letting me in;
My love for you will never expire.
I want you to be yourself no matter what;
Let no one stop you from doing that.
Not even me.

Hey, it's Me...

MY GARDEN

I want you to see the garden inside of me.
Admittedly, I sometimes forget to tend to it;
Parts of it are alive, other parts not so much.
But, I want you to sprint
through my fields of olive;
I want you to twirl among my orchids,
Until dizziness and bliss
are the only things in your body.
Meet my banana trees that feed me at my hungriest,
Make your way to the falls
 that give me drink when I am most dry.
Climb my hills, spotted with bright oleander,
Reach my summit and take in
the warmth that overwhelms me.
Albeit, my climate can change
without difficulty;
Heavy snows can drown my green,
And starless nights can hide all sense of direction.
These instances tend to come and go as they please,
But I have a feeling my garden would sing and flourish
 if you ever come to visit.

Bert Corbeil

Hey, it's Me...

NOW

I'm home in your gaze
Like snow is on trees.
You see my love long before I even have to tell you.

Bert Corbeil

Hey, it's Me...

BABYLON

The fluid of insignificance,
Rattles inside me,
Like a high that would kill a hundred elephants.
Cellar based fantasies
And has-been long shots
Soak in the rusting trumpets of promesse.
Pride and Envy share the wheel,
While Lust and Gluttony fuck in the back,
Packing in as much action
before the sun burns away the pleasure games.

Bert Corbeil

BREATHE & REPEAT

'It'll be okay', I say,
As my mind meets Armageddon.
'Just keep alive', I force the words out,
As my spine feels like it's about to split from my body.
These words have become my ritual,
I repeat them,
Hoping it won't be the last time I say them.

CHILD-LIKE WONDER

We meet at the park outside the school
Where pine cones become crystals,
And swings become rocket-ships.
We hold our breaths rolling down the dew covered hill.
We count all the bugs coming out for lunch
And give them silly names to match their shapes and colors.
We climb to the top of the Everest of slides
Just to sing down its tube, hoping for a harmonizing echo.
Feeling everlasting,
the world past your safety is more lost to me than ever.

Bert Corbeil

RETURNED

The epidermis at the tips of my fingers
Have been scorched off the earth
Through a happy accident
Allowing me to restart my relationship
with the hands of old fellows'.

Your lips are moving with passion,
But I feel abandoned
On this edge of the eighth dimension.

Today's puzzle of the skull
Leaves me dizzy and disappointed
Enough to move on quicker
than my chemicals can handle.

I disconnect unconditionally
Until the high volumes of the night
Return beautifully.

Bert Corbeil

STRANGERS APART

Do you love me,
Or does hurting me just terrify you so?
I look at you
Until your eyes become lakes full of dead beasties,
And your breathing creates craters in my rib cage.
I look at you
And begin to see a ghost of a universe I once set sail in.
To save words,
I sunder our little love
With the hatchet you gifted to me.
Lastly, we are severed forever,
Fated to wander like strangers in familiar places.

DAY ONE

In the city park,
In your hands,
I feel the four seasons from the last ten years,
The Winter at the tip of all your fingers
Cools the embers at the end of your cigarette.
Acres of Summer smooth out your palm,
As the leaves of fall enclose at your wrist.
The little hairs on the back of your hand soften,
Like the needles of the Blue Spruce in Spring.
In the city park,
In your hands,
I feel the four seasons of the next ten years.

Bert Corbeil

WITH NIGHT

The room enters pitch black,
And we become alive.
Sight is abandoned,
But I learn your body by touch,
Where to kiss,
Where to bite,
Where to suck,
I learn what makes us come together.

Bert Corbeil

THE MOON AS A WITNESS

I'm jealous of the moon
When it sheds its light on you,
It reveals every groove and every dint
That paints your body into a wonder beyond comprehension.
It stares down on you
With the purpose to lift you past the stars,
And bring you to your castle of raindrops.
You stare right back at it,
Exhaling all of your thoughts and worries into the night,
Hoping your words bounce off of every rock and star
Until the right one hears you.

Bert Corbeil

I SIT

Wrapped up In the bracelet you made me,
With pinecones on my feet.
I sit in your pupil,
Near the center, where spots of black milk around the brown.
I breathe in your breath
And allow it to settle in my lungs.
Your voice sails it's way through my ears,
Dropping anchor right at the cliffs of my temporal lobe.
Without thought, I begin to lay,
Like an angel in snow.
You soak me in completely,
I venture through your canals and vein,
And leave by means of your mouth.
I embrace your lips once more,
As I sit closer to you than ever before.

Bert Corbeil

A WONDERFUL THING

She comes from Oblivion.
Her whispers are softer than the shores at low tide.
We meet at the branching rocks
where the crabs argue over who to spare next.
Just when I thought I had you figured out,
Your shape changes.
You are a beacon for Life to put its love.
The way you walk between spaces,
Fills my space with magic,
and a high beyond my most pastel fantasies.
You throw my failing attributes into your home,
So I can feel without judgment
While I spend as many seconds as I can with you.
We run in the woods,
And enter a world of screaming ghosts and hurt gods.
Their high heels hit the cobbled courtyard
Harder than lightning striking a lone tree.
Your shape changes yet again,
Into a mossy fig full of grace and choir.
I take a pocketful of pansies
To save as light for when the stars go dark.
I slow my breathing,
To be born again.
I drink what's old,
What's present,

And what comes after,
From a chalice made by my descendants.
You're singing to me,
Like the rivers sing to the ocean.
It's such a wonderful thing to love.

CHANGING DIRECTION

Heading down South
To skid across the clouds
Toward the other end of purgatory.
The blue skies derail into nausea and lunacy.
The leaves spit out mist to secrete any clarity
From the eyes and tongues of the ones passing judgment,
On what little spirit I have slithering around my ribs.

Bert Corbeil

FROLICKING SOULS

Within the torso of the tree,
Moves a parcel of souls
Belonging to entities long forgotten by human kind,
But when the inky night gobbles up most of the light
They slide out from the bosom of the tree
Out to the soirée waiting for them
Over the plains of cobblestone.
When they reach their most merry,
Their chests burst with the most dazzling glow.
At a glance,
They look like specs of lightning frolicking along the shrubs.
They embrace their love for one another,
 By way of only touch and sound.
A human, of mild impression, could easily mistake their love
With the ramblings crickets and owls.
Before slipping back into the caves of the tree,
and their glows wait for the next night,
They leave their marks:
Webs of dust etched into stone and water
As clear as crystals.

AN INSTANT WORTH SAVING

Cover me in kisses,
Like they're tiny new tattoos
That tell a story worth telling,
On my back and between my thighs.
I want to lie in your smell,
Like a bed of smoke.
Break my skin,
Until you drain me dry,
Of everything killing me quicker than I should.
Clench me tight,
I want to become the diamonds
You say live in my iris.
Convince me
My value doesn't have an expiration date,
Fill my arms with a world
We can build around us.
Never say goodbye,
Even if we never meet again.

Bert Corbeil

WHEN AVALON WROTE

To the creature,
who lurks on the knob of land behind my place of comfort,
I see you.
You do not fool me,
Or the human that I service.
We are not friends.
Maybe for a second I thought we were,
But I quickly discarded that notion
after you didn't properly respond to my stare.
I do not appreciate you bringing
 your stench near my place of comfort,
I have made territory here for several fortnights.
You think you can sneak in
Night's shadows as I appease my urine pouch?
False.
For many reasons this is false.
For one, I can sniff danger all the way across a park,
And you are half as far.
For two, wind is my friend.
When I run in it,
I move as fast as car.
Needless to say, it would be wise of you
 to leave this place,
For I will show no mercy if I smell you again.

FOR THE LOVE

Crossing the busy streets of my world,
I only spot heroes.
'Oasis'!
Where the young can grow and the old can breathe.
Miles of miracles spread further inward,
Into the core of believers.
Many more join,
Not out of obligation, but as an invitation.
Upward and onward the ground builds,
Past the clouds and out to the universe.
Neighbors become family,
And friends are found.
Inside homes, ideas of hope crawl up the walls,
And sprout like trees out of the chimneys.
Together we come to refresh
And restart whatever we thought we may have lost.
You and I are the heroes that save the present,
Giving our futures a chance.

Bert Corbeil

THE END OF THE LINE

I stare up at the canyon
From the surface of the sea,
Beneath the river that flows with green.
Thirteen waterways lead to the same end,
Villages where life is less loud and not as bright.
Hundreds of anomalies pour from the cliffs
Into the marrow of the sea.
Childless spirits preach to the too tired to love,
Too tired to unstuck their anchors from the end of the line.
Without a connection,
A second to breathe is what they need.

Bert Corbeil

CRUMBS

You leave crumbs of your existence,
As trails leading to your favorite places.
The swing over the lake,
The narrow ridge blowing kisses at the sky,
The garden of sand filled with towers and valleys,
The easel that collects pieces of you
 like permanent dust bunnies,
The library of our lives that lives in your mind,
And will one day stand in the home on the mountains.
These crumbs never run out,
And will ferment in the earth long past man stomps the land.

Bert Corbeil

GRIMES

You leave crumbs of your existence
As I walk warily to your favorite places.
The swing over the lake,
The narrow ridge, blowing, kisses at the sky,
The garden of sand filled with rocks and valleys,
The easel that collects pieces of you,
The permanent dust bunnies,
The library of your loves that lives in your mind,
And still one day, stand in the name on the mountain,
These crumbs cover the path
And will scream to me of a long past man along the land.

WADING

My tongue wades in your river,
I carry droplets of you down my throat,
Soothing any soreness that existed,
You massage my heart
with the scent of your hair and breath.
In this encounter
The love lives in glory.

Bert Corbeil

WADING

My tongue wades in your river.
I am a molester of ancient mountain
finding any scenes that existed.
You measure my heart
with the scent of your hair and breath
in the encounter
Like low flies in glory.

MEETING AGAIN

You kiss the back of my hand
With earnest,
As if this wasn't the first time
we've encountered one another.
My stare breaks through the falling snow,
Finding what stories glimmer in your eyes.
You feel like an ancient paramour,
That has been fastened in my chest
Long before I could write such words.
I thank the cold, for our embrace,
Allowing for your red to meet my blue,
In a twist of violet ever moving.

Hey, it's Me...

YOUR GREEN PEARLS

We nestle in the lake of our own hair,
You familiarize yourself with the whiskers
that stand on my cheeks.
We climb each other over and over
As if we belong on tree tops.
Shades of green radiate from
the two pearls that sit in your face,
Troves of whispers reveal passages and
pages of your secrets and desires.
Your song turns into a quiet purr
Just as parts of your body start to turn tender.
The moment surpasses the space that holds us,
And we enter a never ending dance of ardency and devotion.

Bert Corbeil

SLEEP LESS

Forcing that wink of sleep
Like it'll be the wink that saves my life,
From this ancient box of needless things
That touches all corners of my body,
Things that shouldn't matter to me
As much as the contents in a lost log of yesteryear.
The dead tree outside my window
Keeps its stare steady and my heartbeat irregular.

Bert Corbeil

DANCING ON AIR

You dance to a piece from nineteen sixty nine,
in your bare feet on the never ending
 carpet covered in the cats' hair.
The book you're reading lays on its belly
on your desk in the overstuffed library,
It takes a break while you go to work
on inspiring the most inner part of my soul.
All this time later you still find ways
past my thorns and pudding.
You're able to sway in the air as if it's instinct,
I kiss your feet to remind you I'm still here.
I climb your aura
To meet where you are,
And reflect in your eyes for just a while longer.

COMPANION

I snuggle in the red of your checks,
Not sure where we're going,
I hang on tight enough
Not to leave a mark.
When need be,
I become your walking stick.
When wanted,
I form into a rock you can rest on.
When you are unable to sing,
I represent your voice with proper sanction.
When you are thirsty,
I am the water that refills you with vigor.
When you are too hot,
I am the wind.
Too cold,
A quilt.
I choose to be at your beck
and call on this journey,
For as long as you want me.
Whether its for miles and miles and miles,
Or until I become too heavy
and you must lighten the load,
I will always sleep with bliss
knowing you are in this world.

Bert Corbeil

COMPANION

I snuggle in the red of your cheeks
Not sure where we're going
I float on light enough
So to leave a mark
When need be.
I became your walking stick
When warped.
I form into a rock you can rest on.
When you are unable to sing,
I represent your voice with proper sanction.
When you are thirsty,
I am the water that refills you with vigor.
When you are too hot
I am the wind
Too cold
A quilt.
I choose to be at your beck
and call on this journey
For as long as you want me.
Whether its fog piles and miles and miles,
Or until I become too heavy
and you must lighten the load.
I will always sleep with I have
knowing you are in this world.

Hey, it's Me...

DRUNK WITH STATIC

I drink alcohol with the moon
Under the garish clouds of winter.
I dip my head back in the frozen pond in the park
To thaw my thoughts,
And find what has me here.
I feel around in the shallows
of the stardust just beneath my skin,
Wondering if there's any reason
 at all for this static state
That has overtaken my luminosity.

Bert Corbeil

Hey, it's Me...

ENDLESS VERSIONS

Hello,
To the version of me
That never left the thick of the forest,
That still lives on the outskirts of the same park,
In the basement of the dead Magnolia tree.
The 'me' who never plans to leave,
Even when the people are no longer recognizable,
Even when they no longer recognize you,
The version of me whose points
 of view will feed their inability,
Whose mind will fail them before
they are acquainted with passion,
Whose promises will die in the
desert of their choosing.
I mourn a life I may never know,
I mourn the version of me that wont ever breathe.
I hold myself and meet the version I will become,
For me, all of me.

Bert Corbeil

LIKE A HOUSE

The blood from my heart
Pours out into the air
Like dust particles in a condemned home.
An attempt at life is made, in earnest,
Even as the walls are drained of color,
As the hallways lose their stepping,
And the animals lose their selves.
I begin to mold and curtail
under the guise of a fruitful renewal,
A tense burst of exertion breaks
the hinges off my front door,
Letting out what little life I had wading in my pipes.

Bert Corbeil

DIFFERENT LANDS

The gates of uncertainty open
with a grin as large as Jupiter,
I inspect the hinges and
wood as if it's gonna prepare me.
With my lapis loafers,
I walk through the thin veil
at the center of the entrance,
The autonomy of the unknown
 curves every part of me,
Sideways and inward.
My teeth turn soft
And my gaze shoots across the new plane
for my existence,
At first see the familiar ruins and scars,
But beyond them lays out beaches
and beaches of sanguinity.
I walk through this eclipse,
And in those sands,
I stay awhile.

Bert Corbeil

DIFFERENT LANDS

The gate of memory flew open
with a whoosh, force of habit,
Long bef the hinges, and
wore as it is a praise put put me
With my lapis necklace,
So well this sign the links on
at the center of the curtain,
With memories of the unknown
surveys every part of me,
Sideways, and inward
My teeth stuck soft,
And my spirit stoops to toss the new plane
for my victim race.
At first see their quieter ripple and worse
But beyond them keep out laughter,
until memories of sunshine,
I walk through time's speed,
And in those sands,
Easily awake.

98

Hey, it's Me...

HOW DOES A FROG FIND ITS HOME

The taste between your legs
Stays with me long after the sheets have been cleaned.
You linger
Among the hairs that grow around my mouth,
At the root of my fingers.
Your touch on my cheek burns sharper
than the scratches you leave on my back.
I linger
On your ankles
Where I've laid my lips,
In your throat,
Like a frog that has found its home.
Our tastes live eternally in the studies of our memories.

Bert Corbeil

AHEAD

Our Future is in the hands of the dreamers
The creators, the doers, the believers
The ones that see the glass half full
The ones that are willing to push and pull
And fight for a better tomorrow
The ones with enough genius to be borrowed
We need to stand up with them,
And stay extant
And make that tomorrow our present

Bert Corbeil

AHEAD

Our Future is in the hands of the dreamers,
The creators, the doers, the believers,
The ones that see the glass half full
The ones that are willing to push and pull
And fight for a better tomorrow
The time with enough go-hut to be borrowed
We need to stand up with them
And say extra *x*
And make that tomorrow our present

102

INITIAL REACTION

When I feel hope moving forward
I know it'll be you.
I feel you right now,
A day you've been gone,
 all I feel is your love.
Your laugh at something inappropriate,
Your tears when your faith in our futures was tested,
Your stubbornness
Your generosity
Your flaws
Your beauty.
Your hope always lives in your children,
We are your legacy.
Your love was always enough
to make our lives worthwhile.

Bert Corbeil

INITIAL REACTION

When I first hope means a reward
I know it'll be one.
I feel you right now.
A day you've been gone
all I feel is your touch.
You laugh at something inappropriate.
Your tears when your child figure hunters, as usual.
Your stubbornness.
Your generosity.
Your anger.
Your bravity.
Your hope shiny lives in your children.
We are our hopes.
Your love was always carrying
to make our lives worth a bit.

I'LL BE WAITING

I'm still waiting
Waiting for you to appear in your bedroom like nothing happened,
Waiting for a moment to scream until my lungs give out,
Waiting for your snores to overrun the hallways another night,
Waiting to be able to piece together what my life will now be,
Waiting to catch up on our lives while we head north on Lake Shore Drive,
Waiting for this bleeding knot in my chest to unfurl itself
Waiting to be with you again.
I'll be waiting.

AIRPLANE THOUGHTS

It hasn't hit me
When I listen to your favorite albums
When I watch movies you loved or would love
When I look at pictures of places you've visited
Or when I hear your voice left on a call
I missed months ago.
When will I realize you are actually gone?
When will I realize you won't be there for my next birthday?
When will I realize our trip to Lake Geneva this year will never happen?
When will I realize I won't see you when I land in Illinois?

Hey, it's Me...

UNORGANIZED GRIEF

My love for you when you were around
Is not the same now that you are gone.
It feels like it is fleeting,
As I grieve what now feels like a distant memory.
Every day I go about the life I lived before your loss
And I feel like I'm losing you.
I feel like I lost you centuries ago.
I was angry at you for too long,
And now that you're gone it only grows,
But it also feels like I have a second chance with you.
I wanted to be like you,
But never exactly like you.
I have your laugh
Your face,
Your love.
I never want your rigid ways,
Or your fractured ideologies that can be seen by future generations.
I want to change forms as I travel across the cosmos,
Where I know I'll see you again,
Our souls will recognize each other like no time has passed.
My love for you will be different then,
But the new love I have found will test the universe in
ways that it will need to ascend to a higher form to carry it.

AN EASY BREEZE

    I burrow my senses deep in the summer that varnishes your hair,
    I don't stop breathing it in until my mind fills with accents of coral.
    You lay on top of me
    Like I'm a favorite bedcover.
    I feel the air in your belly move through you,
    Expelling out like a kiss without lips.
    My chest opens up wide the longer we lay,
    Being sculpted out by every word you fan into my ear.
    Your heart drips onto my ribs,
    A rain that grows flowers on my wooden innards.
    A new earth grows in me,
    One with a breeze that comes with flourishing ease.

Bert Corbeil

AN EASY PRIZE

I burrow my super deep in the summer that scratches sour-
ness,
I don't stop breading it in until, a mind filled with oxygen, I
cord.
You lay on top of me,
Like That floating bathtub.
I feel the air in your belly move through you,
Expecting out like a kiss within him.
My once open mouth wide the longer we lay,
Being sculpted with breath of word you say, to my ear
Your breath drips onto my robe.
A sun that grows flowers on my wooden innards.
A new earth grows in me.
One with a breeze that comes with nourishing tone.

112

CALLED LOVE

I wear my shirt you wore last night like
it's your arms still wrapped around me,
Enfolded in a memory in the making,
One that never ends as long as you call me Love.
Songs grow around us like petals on a flower,
Each one blossoming at a rate thrusted upon us by the stars.
We design notes of pleasure beside our marks of onus.
These songs are never ending in the ages I call you Love.

Bert Corbeil

CALLING LOVE

I wear my shirt you wore last night, like
a young saint, self-wrapped around me,
Enfolded in a memory in the making
One that never ends, as long as you call me Love.
Songs grow around us, like petals on a flower,
Each one blossoming, a rare thread upon us by the stars.
We design notes of pleasure beside our sparks of ours.
These songs are never ending, in the ages I call you Love.

BALANCING EACH OTHER

I fill my mouth
With as much of your hurt and doubts
As you allow me to swallow;
Before my own hurt and doubts spill out of me.
I dig my claws into your velvet thighs,
Squeezing out what ever fluid I can muster,
Invading my thoughts with your light.
I absorb an amount of your flare,
Small enough that it's instantly replenished.

In return I offer you my shade,
Where you can drape yourself
While the world attempts to scorch your life away.
Dip your fevers in the coolness of my dusk,
Sip on the crystal fluxing at my center.
I can be the eclipse that helps stop your light from ever burning out.

THE LIGHT

Is patient,
Is generous,
Is full of more love than any light can carry.
The Light gives me more chances
Then I think I am deserving of.
The Light was planted in a blotchy valley
Where her fires roared against the rock.
As she grew,
She found her way towards light just as bright.
All together
The Light grew.
She grew senses that touch beyond any touchstone.
The Light loves more viscerally
 than any other entity that moves around it,
She holds space for the ones who struggle to keep space.
The Light is resilient in darkness,
And her warmth is absolute.
The Light inspires,
Fans breathe into the ones who don't exhale.
The Light is My Love,
And I will not waste her.

Bert Corbeil

THE LIGHT

I pulled,
Is generous,
Is full of more love than any light can give.
The Light gives me more chances
Than I think I am deserving of.
The Light was planted in a bottle of hay
Where her tiny waited around the rock
As she grows.
She found her way towards light no lengths
All told her
The Light and
The grey stone that touch I voud my own blood.
The Light loves pure, especially
when anything guilty that mere because it
She looks space for the ones who caught up every space
The Light is remote in darkness,
And her warmth is absolute.
The Light inspires,
Fast bhearin into the ones who don't exhale,
The Light is My Love
And I will not want her.

118

Hey, it's Me...

A CONVERSATION WITH MYSELF

Who you are is bigger than any
thought that goes through their head.
Whatever happens happens;
You're bigger than that too.
Every day you live is oh so necessary;
And rewarding.
Real love touches you almost routinely,
You just have to accept its many forms.
People do hear you,
Even if it's not always as apparent as you wish it would be.
There's no need to be desperate for forced love.
You are deserving of the love you give yourself.
And it's okay if you forget that once in awhile,
Just look back on these words for clarity:
You are truly a rarity to humanity,
With a worthy purpose that will conquer
even your biggest insecurity;
The beauty you shower onto others is rooted in you
so deeply that it storms through the earth
 and spreads like wildfire.
And this beauty IS you.

Bert Corbeil

NEW FOLDER

Acknowledgements

To my family and friends, I thank you and I love you more than I am able to express. To everyone who is forever grieving an insurmountable loss, you are not alone.

www.ingramcontent.com/pod-product-compliance
Ingram Content Group UK Ltd.
Pitfield, Milton Keynes, MK11 3LW, UK
UKHW021631110325
456071UK00009B/72